LAUREN ELKIN is a Franco-American writer and translator. Her last book, *Flâneuse: Women Walk the City* was a finalist for the PEN/Diamonstein-Spielvogel Award for the Art of the Essay, a *New York Times* Notable Book of 2017, and a BBC Radio 4 Book of the Week. Her translation, with Charlotte Mandell, of Claude Arnaud's biography of Jean Cocteau, won the 2017 French-American Foundation's Translation Prize. Her next book, *Art Monsters: on Beauty and Excess,* is to be published by Chatto & Windus. She currently lives in London, with her partner and son.

# No. 91/92: NOTES ON A
# PARISIAN COMMUTE

*Lauren Elkin*

Les Fugitives

for bunny, & for s.

'To me, a bus is a big machine for taking pictures, a miraculous tripod to which we attach an imaginary camera, a moving and dynamic tripod.'

—Hervé Guibert, *Ghost Image*

'De l'autobus, je regarde Paris.'

—Georges Perec, *An Attempt at Exhausting a Place in Paris*

The following entries were composed in the Notes app on a yellow iPhone 5c over a period of seven months, from September 2014 to May 2015, while riding the 91 and then the 92 bus in Paris to and from the university where I taught twice a week, and occasionally during other trips on public transport. The goal was to observe the world through the screen of my phone, rather than to use my phone to distract myself from the world. Along the way I thought a lot about how people live together, and experience trauma on an everyday level.

That academic year brought both public and personal grief: the Charlie Hebdo and Hypercacher attacks happened, and then a few months later I lost a pregnancy. The hardest thing to make sense of was how in an instant, the everyday can become an Event. That this could happen to any of us at any time caused me sometimes debilitating anxiety, especially after the attacks of November 13th, which occurred after this project was over but inflect my retrospective reading of it. Looking back to a daily record when you didn't know something massive was coming down the road can be as uncanny an experience as recalling the thing itself; it casts daily life in a dangerous hue, when you thought you were just going about your business.

When the Event is happening, we take to Twitter or watch TV or frantically refresh our news outlets, scanning for something more than the official news, some stray detail that will help us comprehend. It takes time to see the underlying causes, to build a historical narrative. But in the days surrounding it, the Event dwells in a particular space of unknowability.

Over time, the Event weaves into the everyday. People we see on the bus may have been at the Bataclan or know someone who was; the woman in the corner may have had a miscarriage last month. Other people are an immense mystery. We cannot right-click on them and download their history. We do not know where they have been or where they're going. But that they are going together, while companionably ignoring one another, seems of paramount importance.

I believe this is called community.

*Some notes:*

*The 91 goes from Bastille to Gare Montparnasse (and back). The 92 goes from Gare Montparnasse to Porte de Champerret (and back).*

*I get on at Port-Royal Berthollet, change at Place du 18 Juin 1940, and get off at École Militaire (and back).*

*Unless otherwise indicated, mornings are between 8:10 and 8:40. Afternoons are between 1:00 and 5:00, depending on the day.*

*Typing errors and omissions have been preserved where they weren't too disruptive, while others have been corrected for clarity.*

**first semester**

22/09/14

Monday morning

Too early it's too early I hate morning classes I should not teach them. Even after a quick dribble from the Nespresso machine I'm not quite myself. I've got a seat on the inside next to the window. I lean my head against it and study anything with words printed on it. The map with the 91 bus route as it crawls along the Boulevard Montparnasse. A poster announcing an upcoming strike and consequent bus diversion. Encouragements, not threats, to validate your tickets. I look around at my fellow passengers. They seem calm in the knowledge that they have validated their tickets as they stare at the screens of their phones, little wells of blue glowing in the thick dark of morning. Tapping and swiping, tapping and swiping.

A sign published by the RATP gives advice:

Your telephone is precious. It may be envied. We recommend vigilance when using it in public.

I look down at my own phone. It is precious (it was expensive). I will take their advice. I will be vigilant when using it. I will carry out a public transport vigil, and use my phone to take in the world around me, to notice all the things I would miss if I were using it the way I have been, the way they all are. I'll use the phone to look around me rather than down at its screen. Instead of taking pictures that wind up in someone else's morning feed, I'll use the phone to see the world myself. Exercises not in style but in vigilance.

I type as fast as I can and sort out the autocorrect later.

22/09/14

Monday afternoon

On the Boulevard du Montparnasse is a store called L'espace tabac, tobacco space. We go past it every day on the bus. L'espace tabac in the morning, l'espace tabac in the afternoon. L'espace tabac going one way; l'espace tabac the other. I remember when Paris was all tobacco space. Now it's contracted to this one store. Out of the corner of my eye I see a man who seems to be petting an invisible animal, as if he were miming the animal being there, defining the shape of it in the air with his caressing hand. I look at him directly and it's his suede ankle boot he's touching, running his hand over the silken piles.

25/09/14

Thursday morning

Leaning against the pole, in a stoned sleepy stupor. Awakened by mewing – someone's brought their cat on the bus in rush hour. An early morning appointment at the vet? a needy feline who can't be left alone? I wish I could bring my dog to school but we'd all be so distracted we'd get nothing done and they're not paying all that money to hang out with a small furry creature. There's a time and a place for a dog. A guy sitting in the row in front of me is reading long text messages and I wonder what are they about? Professional, personal, a break-up, intricate dinner plans?

25/09/14

Thursday afternoon

A woman's saying the rosary a woman's putting on lipstick a woman's composing music on her MacBook with some kind of program I'd like to know more about, humming and snapping and holding her headphones close to her head. A man's listening to his headphones so loudly I hear all the details of the chanson, down to the lyrics, words that are well-adapted to our ballet of comings and goings, all our gettings-on, all our gettings-off. I'm exhausted. Teaching hard and not sleeping well. I mixed up Hunger Games with Divergent in a student conference today. Oh the shame.

et mon amourette / qui était trop jolie / vers d'autres conquêtes / bientôt repartie

and my little fling / who was far too fine / off she went stealing / other hearts than mine

29/09/14

Monday morning

Place du 18 Juin 1940. Waiting for the 92. Stopped for coffee at Starbucks. Made up a little ditty to keep myself company as I crossed the street. Got my cof-fee/Got my cof-fee/Gonna drink it/drink my cof-fee. The bus will be here in 5 minutes. I may be late. The other day when I was here waiting for the bus a woman asked me if her scarf looked ok. I told her yes yes it did, and quivered with joy at having been mistaken for a French girl who might know anything about scarves. Then I worried there was something wrong with her scarf, something I couldn't see, and that someone at her work would notice and either not tell her, and judge her for it, or tell her, and then she would think back to what I said, and revise her opinion of me.

29/09/14

Monday afternoon

Oi. Manspreader. Bouge ton cul.

People get so into their phones they forget where they are. That they're in public and that there are other people around who might want to SIT DOWN

What is it about the bus that makes people not want to read the newspaper or a book but only their phones. Down below they still read on paper. Up here on the surface it's only screens.

Move your ass

02/10/14

Thursday morning

In the early sunlight the sea foam green sign on the 21's forehead glows gold, as if it were passing for another bus, the yellow 83 perhaps. Maybe at night when we're all asleep the buses sneak out and try each other's routes. At any rate neither of these buses is my bus. In the morning rush to work the world is a little messy. A Mercedes has climbed up on the sidewalk and waits there, its blinkers on; the car seems to know it's doing something not quite right; people of all ages scoot by on those razor things and sometimes they scoot into other people and everyone is grouchy but they move on quickly. There is much rushing across streets to make the light, especially from me, as you never know when the 91 bus might be lurking just down the road, ready to rush up the minute you're stuck waiting to cross the street. This morning I make the light, and sure enough the bus is approaching, almost empty. The magical mythical 8:12. I have made the magic bus. Almost as hard to catch as the cat bus in My Neighbor Totoro.

Neko no basu!

02/10/14

Thursday afternoon

Received a spam email with the subject line 'Devolve, Gilmar!'

Thinking about what it means to be asking to be French because I have my citizenship interview tomorrow. Why do I want to be French? Who the hell knows? Because I've lived here for years and still have to go to the prefecture once a year, or every couple of years, and provide all the papers, only to find I'm short this one or that one. The anxiety of those encounters, being judged and found wanting, guilty of the offense of not making the right photocopies. And by this time I think I'm almost the last of my American friends not to have married a French person or found some job to sponsor me. I remain unaffiliated, or otherwise affiliated. I just want to be able to stay here and not to be hassled, not to be judged on my photocopies. and it would be nice to be able to vote. To have some say in things however small.

Evolve, Elkin!

06/10/14

Monday morning

Wtf are these Americans doing on my early morning commute and why do they I mean we talk so loud is it because we're shouting to be heard across the plains? Because we're not used to having neighbors? Have we struggled as a nation to build ourselves a place where we can talk as LOUDLY AS WE LIKE and then take it on the road, as a national characteristic?

This woman is telling a story like she's a barker at the carousel.

06/10/14

Monday afternoon


I've brought Jacques Roubaud's bus book with me to read. Thank goodness I write prose and don't have to worry about alexandrines. But then my language is more pedestrian ha ha. No time for wordplay, we're commuting here and I'm doing the best I can. Instead of wordplay timeplay. Phoneplay.

Roubaud's on the 29. All the buses that leave from Saint-Lazare start with a 2. All the buses that leave from Montparnasse start with a 9. I'm on the other end of his proposition. I didn't know this about numbers. 91 to the 92. 92 to the 91. Twice a week. Without even thinking.

Wikipedia, loading, loading, part-loaded, scroll, scroll, got it.

Line 91. First operated on 12th November 1945. The line runs from 6 am to 1 am Monday through Saturday, and 7 am through 1 am on Sundays and holidays.

It connects three train stations:

Montparnasse
Gare d'Austerlitz
Gare de Lyon

(Which is why there are always people
with suitcases.)

Six hospitals:

Saint-Vincent-de-Paul
Baudelocque
Cochin
Val-de-Grâce
Pitié-Salpêtrière
Quinze-Vingts

(How many of these people are sick?)

And connects with eighteen other bus lines.

I'll leave that list to another day.

09/10/14

Thursday morning

Everyone's up and out already and I join them this morning, the guy in the chair upholstery shop is there with the chairs, the guy in the caterers is there receiving deliveries, I walk past a man entering a porte-cochère who drops his cigarette butt as I walk by and the smell of the tobacco wafts up to me and for a moment mingles with the cold morning air and it's like a proof of life. You don't want to get a lungful of it: just a whiff of someone else's smoke, as the spark goes out. I'm glad all these people are out here doing what they're doing, and my bus comes and I perch on a backwards-facing seat. Really annoyed by people who sit on the outside seat leaving the inside one empty. Unless you have a physical inability to slide over, slide the hell over! Even if you're getting off soon! The person who sits on the outside will understand. It is their responsibility to understand and to get up for you, just as it is your responsibility to move over for them. Bus ethics people – give it a try.

09/10/14

Thursday afternoon

There's a scruffy guy lounging over two seats who is clearly not interested in sharing so I sit somewhere else. Then an elderly man gets on and says excuse me, may I sit here please and the young scruffy guy gets up and mutters casse-couilles, putain.

By the door, as I wait for my stop, a man in a hat looks out the window and says 'sarkozy'.

fucking pain in the ass

13/10/14

Monday morning

Too early. Too dark. Hate Mondays. You can't Instagram how hot it is on this bus. I'm sitting backwards and getting nauseous and want to close my eyes but that makes it worse. The woman sitting across from me practices piano fingering on her handbag. It's one of those Gérard Darel bags everyone had in 2007. I stare at the military details on a woman's jacket. I don't like them. When I saw her from the back I thought wow nice coat because it's a nice thick great wool and in the back it's cut well, like a man's coat, but actually there are cutesy pockets with piping and epaulettes and wrist straps. Downright gaudy. But from the back she looks smart, capable, interesting. Oh god there's a zipper.

13/10/14

Monday afternoon

At the stop where I change. A bus pulls away to reveal a distinct order written on the side of a post-office truck. Faites vos achats sur internet, c'est moi qui livre vos paquets. I clamber into a seat and move aside the coat of the man sitting next to me to keep from sitting on it. Excusez-moi I say politely. I have a headache. He is wearing too much cologne. When this man gets off the bus I notice his head is completely bald under his blue woolen beanie. Not the kind of bald that comes naturally for some men with age. I don't know how I know he's been sick, it's just something I feel I know.

Shop online, I'll deliver your parcels

16/10/14

Thursday morning


What is that guilt, when you're sitting and other people are standing, and you think maybe they have more of a right to sit than me, I have no way of knowing, but then maybe I have more of a right to sit than they do, and I got here first, but can that really be the ultimate decider, I got here first? We haven't evolved any more subtle way of resolving this so I can feel like less of an asshole sitting in this seat on the bus looking at these women with dyed hair red hats pulled down jackets puffy age indeterminate they might be only a little older than me or they might be decades older.

I keep catching up with the older women.

18/10/14

Saturday afternoon

Mom with three kids, two in a stroller (twins?). Third one kicking repeatedly against the bench in the bus shelter. The same bench I'm sitting on. I grin and bear it out of solidarity. Three kids. Must be tough. Helped by science, the last pregnancy? (She looks much older than me and I'm long overdue myself.) A surprise split in the cells, or whatever happens so you see new mothers of 42 with triplets (The third 21 and still no 91). The kid is now tugging on the wire that makes up the 'back' of the bench so people don't have to lean against the actual bus shelter. Every time he yanks on the wire I'm thrust forward. By the third time I lean forward in advance. (Fourth 21.) I cast a gently irritated glance at the mother. She's too busy texting to notice what her kid is doing. One of the stroller children has a bloody gash on its nose. She eventually notices and touches it to see if it's wet. It is. She wipes her finger on her jeans and checks the kid's fingernails. They're the culprit: jagged as anything. Also it's freezing out and they're not wearing mittens. But maybe she's very busy and forgot to trim their nails and forgot the mittens. (I have been waiting for this bus for a half hour. I get up and stand at the front of the line. I damn well better get a seat after a half hour.) I consult my own phone, wondering if I'll be too busy to cut my own kid's fingernails one day, and how do you cut them anyway so they're not sharp, and I have an image of myself using a nail file on my newborn and that doesn't seem right either, maybe you just keep them in mittens til they're twelve and that way you'll never forget them. I look at the woman again and she's pulled out a cigarette. An hour later I pass the same woman and children on the Rue Guynemer.

20/10/14

Monday morning

Priority given to those who wish to close the windows, it says on the bus wall. Who decides these things? Child wearing a wolf hat with two long fabric pieces hanging down on each side, ratty white and pilling, dirty at the bottom. Observatoire-Port Royal and there's a big push to get off; I end up sitting not because I want to sit so much as it's the best way to get out of the way but now that I'm here I'm glad for the seat and guilty at the same time

20/10/14

Monday afternoon

A woman being harassed by a ticket
agent. Apparently she didn't buzz in her
Navigo pass. the machine on the right was
broken. The ticket agent thinks she should
have tried the one on the left. 'But I pay
my bills every month!' she protests force-
fully. 'I pay my fare! What does it matter if
I touch in?' It matters. Her African accent
and dress work against her. He's trying
to give her a ticket. They're still arguing
three stops later when I get off

23/10/14

Thursday morning

This window is the only thing keeping me upright. How am I going to teach Mrs Dalloway in this state? I think of looking at the book, as if the familiar opening paragraphs would jolt my brain into a functioning state. But I can't be bothered. Now I understand why my elementary school teachers always stank of coffee and cigarettes. The older you get, the more you have to soak yourself in stimulants to function in the morning

23/10/14

Thursday afternoon

God this bus is slow we've been crawling up the same stretch of boulevard for 15 minutes I can't bear it, I want to get home already put my feet up have a snack watch some TV kiss the dog. One Haussmann-ian building every couple of minutes. A Parisian way of measuring speed.

27/10/14

Monday morning

Girl on the bus with thin bony hands, a thick gold ring on one middle finger. Dark hair, cut in bangs, mulberry lipstick. I envy her. What does she see when she looks in my direction? My little boy hands? Dyed blond hair, lipstick too red for this hour? She looks natural and pretty. But her roots will go soon enough, and then she'll be next to me at the salon.

27/10/14

Monday afternoon

Reading The Years and this quote is good for that Zadie article I have to write. 'The omnibus in which she had come, with its silent passengers looking cadaverous in the blue light, had already vanished'. Woolf's usually so humanizing to the people on public transport but this sounds like she's been reading The Waste Land, I had not thought death had undone so many, Zadie is much more human about the people on the bus, much more Mr Bennett and Mrs Brown, all novels start with an old lady in the carriage opposite. Something's jiggling my arm. Jiggle jiggle jiggle. I look down. It's the child in the seat next to me tapping away on a little red blackberry. I assume it's a game he's playing, I can't really tell, the sunlight makes a glare on his screen. How old is he? Not more than 9?

30/10/14

Thursday morning

Your glittery sandals are awful but the rest of your outfit is good.

30/10/14

Thursday afternoon

The bus is on diversion and all hell is breaking loose.

— But – but – where's he going?

— What's he doing?

— What's going on?

— The fuck is he doing?

The foment builds and builds and I think they might rush the driver in his seat up there so he agrees to stop in unexpected places on this unexpected route. But he can't stop just anywhere. He has to stop somewhere safe. This doesn't matter to the woman who wants to get off right now right here and not a little ways down and for whom it is becoming increasingly urgent to get off right away no rightaway:

— Can I get off here? Or here? Or here? MONSIEUR IL FAUT QUE JE DESCENDE LÀ LÀ LÀ LÀ LÀ

SIR I HAVE TO GET OFF HERE HERE HERE HERE HERE

03/11/14

Monday morning

Poetics of the city as viewed through the bus. The only time you're at this height. Not as high as a first floor but higher than the ground. You never move quickly. It's not like a car; there's no weaving no darting just a progression of stops and starts. You're always going forward. The 91, then the 92, making its way along the long boulevards, which curve north or south but never turn. The only time you see the city at this pace. You think you have a moment to take a quick picture of a caryatid, a poster, yourself reflected in the windows of the building, but just as soon as you've tapped and swiped over to the camera setting on the phone, the bus is moving again.

06/11/14

Thursday morning

Nearly there, Invalides slides up outside the window the phone picks up a song on shuffle come with me go places I can't listen to this album without thinking of this guy I knew once well that was years ago time to take back the new pornographers. a woman is reading a tall thin Actes Sud paperback she's covered over with pink paper.

06/11/14

Thursday afternoon

Catch up with email, catch up with Twitter, catch up with Facebook, catch up with Instagram, catch up with Pinterest, catch up with email. Catch up with Twitter, catch up with Facebook, catch up with Instagram, catch up with Pinterest, catch up with email, catch up with Twitter. Catch up with Facebook, catch up with Instagram, catch up with there's nothing new on Pinterest

10/11/14

Monday morning

Girl nattering away on phone in too-close proximity. Tempted to read aloud from book I'm reading about Woolf's essays. Eh ben moi tu sais je ne voulais pas qu'elle me dise ce qu'il faut faire j'étais comme toi t'es qui tu me prends pour qui je savais pas quoi dire j'étais comme – ben tu vois c'est n'importe quoi tu vois tu vois and on and on. Woman leaning against the pole has her jacket misbuttoned, one panel hangs lower than the other, who will tell her? I see the same mother with her two kids boy and girl who I see a lot if I catch the 8:12. Someone bumps my knees climbing over me to get to the inside seat. I would have moved if they'd asked. Thinking about how it took time to learn how to ride the bus in Paris, my friends mostly don't take the bus, they say it stresses them out, me too I get stressed when I don't know where to find the bus stop. But my bus stop to go to school is easy to find, right in the middle of the Boulevard Port-Royal. If I need to know which bus to take to get somewhere else I ask the RATP website. Their app is kind of shit. And they replaced all the bus stops one by one and installed fancy new LED signs that are supposed to tell you how long til the next bus comes but of course they never work.

Well, you know, I didn't like her telling me what I was supposed to do, you know? I was like, who are you, who do you think I am, I didn't know what to say, I was like – you know? what even is that, you know?

17/11/14

Monday morning

Reading Species of Spaces. Why have I never noticed before how much Perec likes the word 'parallelepiped'? Every time I teach Perec I'm more convinced I need to teach an entire class on his work. The way he sees the world, his awareness of how difficult it is to really 'see' it, what does it mean to 'see' it, when we can only see bits and pieces of it. When we go to new cities we climb up to high places to try to see it all at once, to take it all in as a whole; Perec goes to his café and writes the city bit by bit piece by piece. Someone on Facebook: I know this is annoyingly vague, but if any of you were planning to be mean to me this week i'd appreciate it if you'd put it off awhile. Too much bad news, sorrow, etc. This is a person who has only ever been a competitive back-stabbing – I fight the impulse to use a misogynist slur. I board the 92.

20/11/14

Thursday morning

Blue tutu Chanel bag fake lashes girl you look amazing.

20/11/14

Thursday afternoon

Taught Perec today. An Attempt at Exhausting a Place in Paris. The kids were into it. They liked thinking about how the place we look at the world from shapes the way we see it. At first they're bogged down by all the details. They've never read anything like it. They're used to stories, with plots, and characters, or textbooks. They haven't encountered writing like this, writing of the everyday, writing without an argument, writing that suggests, that counts, that tracks. Tomorrow I'll take them to Saint-Sulpice and they'll do the exercise for themselves, and see how tough it is to notice everything, and how freeing it is to try.

The one thing they notice are the buses. Perec tracked all the buses that went through the Place Saint Sulpice those few days in 1974. I never noticed the buses so much said one student but now everywhere I go in the city I'm keeping track of them. Another was like but why does he do this, I don't understand, who does this, who reads this? I didn't know how to answer her. that book strikes me as less a means of writing for someone, and more a means of making sense of the world. Like: things are out of control. Slow down. Count the buses. Pattern the world.

24/11/14

Monday morning

That feeling in the back of my throat, like it's rusting. Crap I hope I'm not getting sick. I listen to a France Inter podcast but I'm too tired to make out the subject. Something about bees? Or abbeys.

24/11/14

Monday afternoon

Oh whoops think I was just guilty of #womanspreading: when your bag verges onto the seat next to you subtly discouraging anyone from sitting down

## 01/12/14

## Monday morning

Neon green numbers spray painted on the pavement, number ones formed European-style with hooks, like runes. I have a bad cough. I run for the bus with a mother and her daughter. We all make it. I get something slick on my hand when I hold the bar to help me into a seat. I tell myself it's someone else's hand cream. (This is what I tell myself.) From the corner of my eye it looks like the girl next to me is knitting. I turn my head to see what and realize she's de-tangling her earphones. She plugs them into her ears, one by one. I plug in my own. In front of me the mother fixes her daughter's pony-tail. We all cough. I lean back, and close my eyes, my blood still heavy with sleep. If I'm not careful I'll miss my stop.

01/12/14

Monday afternoon

A woman bends over to pick up a penny, that is, a centime, from the floor. A man flips a folded-up piece of pink paper back and forth. A petite woman wears an olive green wool cape. She looks like Peter Pan. A man wears a grey puffer jacket. He looks like the Michelin Man. Brown socks silver shoes. A nun texting. There are charms dangling from her phone but I can't tell what they are. Neither is a cross. Someone offers her a seat and she doesn't take it. Some elderly people with canes get on and there is much discussion about where to seat them and who is getting off where and it is all resolved in a very fair and civilized manner. When it is my turn to get off I croak excusez-moi madame to the woman in front of me who was one of the key judges determining the previous solution. I want to be polite to her to show that I too am fair and civilized and well-brought-up. But my voice betrays me. It's rough and uncouth, the voice of fatigue and illness, the uncontrollable, the abject. I am a bit more body than mind. I walk a few paces and overtake a man with a cane. I turn the corner and stop to make these notes. As I lean and write, the man with the cane overtakes me.

04/12/14

Thursday morning

Late for my first class. Slept right through my alarm. Coughing it up and no where to spit it. In public that is.

08/12/14

Monday morning

It's 8:30 am and there is a woman in business attire crunking on the bus. I wish I could film her but I don't want to be rude.

When my alarm went off it was pitch black outside. What happened to daylight savings? I never remember from one year to another how dark it gets in the morning in winter. I guess we forget it, like pain. I haven't been up this early in a while I don't think I'll stop for coffee today. I really don't feel well. Rufus Wainwright spins out of the random selector in the jukebox in my hand, my jukebox-phone. La lune trop pale caresse l'opale de tes yeux blasés. I've never managed to get inside that song, not in those nights living at the foot of Montmartre, not in all the nights I've spent wandering the streets that trellis uphill, maybe once or twice I came close in the bar at the top of the stairs the one with all the black and white photographs glued to the exposed beams in the ceiling. I step off the bus and the air is gentle though it's cold out, it feels like it does when I get off the plane at CDG and I feel the difference in whatever it is that makes this France and I know I'm home. Bad perfume and a cigarette. Good perfume and a cigarette. Ladies you're killing me.

Too pale is the moon caressing the opal of your uncaring eyes

08/12/14

Monday afternoon

one of those winter days when everywhere smells of soup. the world is full of
buses and I am always on them. the buses
are starting to get to me. I have to give
that talk on zadie smith and I think I'll
do it on that thatcher quote what was it
again? something about being a loser for
taking the bus after 30 I'm 36 maggie t
would have no use for me at all

11/12/14

Thursday morning

Little kids two of them staring up at the announcement board calling out all the bus times. 91! 4 minutes! 83! 6 minutes! 26! 99! 7 minutes! a hundred minutes! Impossible numbers, impossible routes mixed with actual numbers, actual routes. It's a long wait today. I look at my watch anxiously and wonder at how light the sky is. As we trail down to the end of the year I thought the dark would lengthen on both ends, morning and night. The world outside looks like it's been passed thru an Instagram filter the darks are darker the stone more wet

17/12/14

Wednesday afternoon

gave them their final exam and now I'm
weighed down with little blue exam books
and their final essays my bag is cutting
into my shoulder but there's nowhere to
sit. thank goodness the semester is over
and we're going away to the jura for a
long weekend, I am going to sit with the
dog in front of the fireplace in our hotel
and mark papers as it goes dark outside,
they will bring me mugs of cocoa and
glasses of wine and I won't have to run
after any more buses for a while.

second semester

20/01/15

Tuesday morning

We're all thinking the same thing, it's the first day back to work since it all happened and it feels like we swallowed something down the wrong pipe and we're just starting to be able to take regular breaths again we came out of our houses ok I came out of my house and we marched in defiance but the defiance has taken a backseat to our commute as we try to get on with things even though there are seventeen fewer Parisians than there were this time last week

23/01/15

Friday morning

What are we doing?

27/01/15

Tuesday morning

People get on and off as we wend our way. For a while there's no one across from me and I can put my feet up on the hump where the wheel is, under the seat in front of me. I take them down when someone comes. Now there are people standing in the aisle. L'heure de pointe is what they call it but there's nothing pointy about rush hour, just a press, warm people pressed against each other's bodies, like some kind of word-less woolly love-in. I guess we need each other. People are dressed too warmly for the weather. It's pretty warm for January but we're all wearing scarves and fur hats as if a Siberian wind were blowing.

#jesuischarlie giving way on twitter to #jenesuispascharlie.

rush hour

30/01/15

Friday morning

I keep crying in buses

30/01/15

Friday afternoon

The driver pulls up next to a puddle. People descend in an ungainly fashion – the step is too high for most – and try not to step in it. Over to the curb is too far.

03/02/15

Tuesday morning

Girl from behind, the silhouette of the 2010s: topknot, thick scarf very thick round the neck, roomy drop-shoulder black wool coat. She is everywhere. In fact she looks like my friend H. I lean over a little to see the shoes. (I could recognize this friend by her shoes.) How funny it would be to see H on the bus on the way to work! But what would she be doing on this bus she doesn't live in the part of town where they start with nines, she's over where they start with fours. Black ankle boots, no heel. I start to say her name. But the thighs are different. Not her then

03/02/15

Tuesday afternoon

A bus that is not my bus pulls up, then pulls away. On its back is an advertisement for the television show Un village français, about the Second World War, which has just started airing its new season. Il va falloir être résistant, it says.

Resistance will be necessary

06/02/15

Friday morning

Sometimes I leave the house and without warning the buses aren't running. Taxi! Or no: that is a twentieth-century sound, the twenty-first century slides silently like this: tap swipe swipe tap tap tap, and my Uber pulls up. Slow drive thru the 7th (at the rate of 2 Haussmanns per 5 minutes). Fancy locals walking their children to school. Women in black stockings and heels. Hair up. Men in suits, more rare. Money on their feet and in their hair and faces. The car stops in front of my school and I look like all the other children of the 7th arrondissement being dropped off by drivers in black cars with tinted windows.

06/02/15

Friday afternoon

AHHHHHHHHLAAAAAAALAAAAAAAAA
HUH HUH
AHHHHHHHHLAAAAALAAAAAAAAAHUH
AHHHHUUUUHHHAAAHUUUUUGGHH
HHHHHH

(Keening child)

10/02/15

Tuesday afternoon

On the 28 today just for a change. So many sweet little old ladies on this bus. Not enough seats to give up for them. It goes past our old apartment at 59 avenue de saxe. There are bits of white tape on all the windows. Has mme drouin sold? Or has she just installed new windows? I couldn't really see anything in my old room on the second floor except the open doorway into the hallway. In that room I cried with jetlag and missed my family, the furthest away from them I'd ever been, and read Wally lamb into the wee small hours of the morning. Later I would switch rooms with Shannon and she would have loud sex in there with her visiting boyfriend who was two years younger than us so we called him the fetus.

13/02/15

Friday morning

I just miss my bus. It pulls away from the curb then gets stuck at the light. I think about knocking on the door to plead with the driver then I don't do it. I feel like I'm jinxed when it comes to these buses. They don't come for a long time and when they do it's right after you'd want them to.

13/02/15

Friday afternoon

These young girls took the bus one stop
from école militaire to duroc. Why? Where
are they going? What are these lives that
live in such increments, between one stop
and another? They are incomprehensible
to me. As I type this a guy brushes past
me dramatically although there is plenty
of room to go around me. My own path
today is a collection of specific tasks tied
to people and creatures. I had to pick up
my check I had to get a croissant I had to
shop for my niece I have to get medicine
for my dog these are the needs that give
logic to my trajet. What is theirs? Thinking
of Debord and that young girl who only
moved between three points in Paris. Let
that never be me. Let me always venture
out of my triangle, out of my bounds.

journey

20/02/15

Friday morning

Made the bus today instead of taking a cab. Feels virtuous, like going to the library. Actually it's a good workout running for them, changing, walking to work from the bus stop. The kind of workout you can do while eating a croissant. I've been spending too much money anyway. Went to see a lawyer the other day because they turned down my citizenship request, again. Last time it was because I was a graduate student and didn't have a full-time job. Votre situation est trop instable they said. This time they cited my lack of a full-time work contract. Votre insertion professionnelle est incomplète they said. Bollocks the lawyer said, well n'importe quoi is what she said, you're a writer. You've published books. How much more inserted can you be. There is no full-time contract for writers.

The words they choose always amuse me. Unstable like I'm a wobbly table. Incomplete insertion like I'm an ATM card someone put in wrong.

20/02/15

Friday afternoon

The mark of the non native speaker – I
can't hear why dégueulasse is more offensive and dirtier than dégoûtant but it is,
a mother just chastised her daughter for
saying it the same way an ex-boyfriend
once chastised me and here I am standing
because the only available seat is next to
a man so smelly I had to stand back up
and that is so fucking dégueulasse not to
mention offensive.

24/02/15

Tuesday morning

Someone drops their mobile, bends over to pick it up, drops it again. Thought of a bus story E told me. E was leaving a building where she was looking for an apartment. On her way out of the lobby she was jostled by a young boy running out of the building. As he bumped into her something fell to the floor. She thought it was her mobile that he had tried to steal. But as she picked it up, gathering the phone, the battery pack, the piece of plastic that holds the battery in, she saw that it was his. She ran out to find him and saw him sprinting towards a bus. She ran faster to try to catch him. He got on. The doors closed but the driver saw her running. She made it on and cried did someone drop a mobile? And the boy said I did! And the driver said t'as de la chance.

you're in luck

24/02/15

Tuesday afternoon

I'm reading Hervé Guibert. In the middle of his book on photography he has a chapter about buses. It's as good a way to view the city as another. Better, even. You're on the move. Taking it all in. Slightly above all the congestion it clears our sight like menthol clears our sinuses – it is at the same time a tracking shot, a boom, and a pan. Pan out. Fan across. Two little blond boys playing with water guns on a wraparound balcony shoot at a man on the ground but he likes it and only pretends to yell at them.

27/02/15

Friday morning

Have fallen into the dead zone between
91 buses. It's rush hour but they're in
no rush. One bus every 8 minutes suits
them fine.

10/03/15

Tuesday morning

Back from spring break and I feel like crap. Today is a day when after weeks of terrible air pollution you can't see the Eiffel Tower in the haze and they have forbidden cars with even-numbered license plates from driving in Paris. And they've made public transport free. Some people haven't heard and they put their Navigo passes against the machines and it makes a rude noise and glows red. They think their passes don't work or maybe the machines. No one tells them. But there are so many people. A woman with a cane doesn't want to sit down when a girl offers her seat. To climb up and back down is toute une histoire she says, you have no idea, and anyway I'm getting off at the next stop. At the next stop she does and so does the girl and her friend and I take the seat near the window but even though there are so many people no one sits next to me, maybe it's apparent I'm getting sick. They ought to circulate more buses if they want everyone to take them.

Look at all the smug drivers on the street with their odd-numbered license plates. Impaire. Unpaired. Every so often someone with an even license plate. They'll get a fine if they're caught. And meanwhile rumbles in my stomach and lower abdomen and the chills and oh god this is horrible and I'm late because even though there are fewer cars the bus takes just as long

such a fuss

17/03/15

Tuesday morning

No seats on the bus today and I think I'm pregnant. But I prefer to stand.

20/03/15

Friday afternoon

Suddenly the world is full of strollers. I pay attention to the way the parents angle them up and into the buses, I take note of who goes where, how they slide into their parking spaces, how the parents hit the brake to immobilize them, how they keep their kids quiet, how they stop them licking the walls of the bus. There are so many things to know now.

24/03/15

Tuesday morning

So far not a single man has given up his
seat for me, my friend J said when she
came to town, six months pregnant. The
only people who stand for me are women.

24/03/15

Tuesday afternoon

I'm exhausted from growing a human and the buses are slow. Couldn't wait 14 min for the next 92 so I jumped in a cab. It follows my bus all the way home. I get off at my stop.

25/03/15

Wednesday afternoon

Sometimes I get the bus for one stop now. I lean against the railing in the handicapped area and contemplate this new reality. Everything smells so intense like it's all been sprayed with a perfume of its own scent, like the smells are in high definition, if high definition could make you want to hurl

26/03/15

Thursday morning

Paris sent la merde ce matin pas vrai?

Paris smells like shit this morning don't you think?

26/03/15

Thursday night

There are a lot of people on the tram!

27/03/15

Friday morning

#sympathyjoyandfellowfeelingofbus
pausingforsomeonerunningtocatchthebus

#annoyanceofthebuspausingtowaitfor
someonerunningtocatchit

#anguishofrunningtomakethebusand
missingit

#satisfactionofrunningtocatchthebusand
makingit

27/03/15

Friday afternoon

This bus is on diversion. The driver breaks
the fourth wall to tell us. Then so do the
passengers, consulting and commiserat-
ing with each other whereas ten minutes
ago they pretended they were invisible.
All of us departing from convention.

31/03/15

Tuesday morning

You never see people begging on the bus. Taking the bus you only see a certain kind of person. There are some women who just to look at them makes you think they smell like cigarettes and heavy secret smells and would get eye makeup all over your pillow. These women I often see on the bus.

31/03/15

Tuesday afternoon

The bus is full and I have to stand. A little girl is standing next to me, her head at my hip. She looks up at me, then begins to play with a frayed place on the thigh of my jeans. She's singing a little song that goes hello hello then I can't understand the rest of the words. She looks up to see if I mind her playing with the loose threads on my jeans. Hello! I say brightly in English, and scare her.

01/04/15

Wednesday afternoon

Girls using the bendy part of the bus as a jungle gym. They stick their feet in the accordion part and hoist themselves up with their arms till they're parallel to the ground. Then one does this while the other slips underneath her making a table of her back, then slowly rises up. They wouldn't dare this in rush hour.

03/04/2015

Friday morning

When did absolutely everyone get pregnant? No one ever used to be. Now they all are. The word pregnant is different now, I think I'll never use it metaphorically again, not that I ever really did, though I do like my pauses, pregnant or otherwise

03/04/15

Friday afternoon

A pregnant woman tries to get on but another woman nearly throws her off the step in her hurry to get on the bus first. She finally makes it on but the only open seat is inhabited by a woman's bag. The pregnant woman is able to make her move it but only with effort. The woman thinks her bag needs her seat more than a woman with a soccer ball for a stomach.

07/04/15

Tuesday morning

The morning thumb ballet of checking all the things I check on my phone now includes reading these emails telling me what kind of legume I'm growing. Poppy seed, sesame seed, lentil.

it's spring, you can feel it coming on so subtle

07/04/15

Tuesday afternoon

Sitting on a bench. So much teaching. So many hormones. A strange combination. Things they say in class sometimes bring an unexpected tear to my eye. Or I get choked up when I tell them how it makes me sad when they plagiarize. Such a feeling of relief to see the bus round the corner. My hero.

10/04/15

Friday morning

we're moving soon and I won't be taking this bus anymore. I'll be taking the metro. And in a month I won't be teaching at this school anymore. I hope I'll have a job at another school, a permanent job, a real job. If I don't I'll just work on my writing till the baby comes. That would be nice too. Everything is about to be hard but so nice.

10/04/15

Friday afternoon

It should be illegal to wear perfume on public transport.

And to eat crisps.

14/04/15

Tuesday morning

The impatience and the having to wait of pregnancy.

This will teach you time.

14/04/15

Tuesday afternoon

I pretty much had to yank the iPhone out of this dude's hands to get him to look up long enough to let me through to the inside seat. This is public space in the age of the cell phone. Rare bus today – he and I are the only people I can see looking at screens.

So many women in black and white striped marinières. And I'm one of them.

Oh now I see two people both men on their phones plus us.

A kid reads Astérix matin. Is that like the Daily Goblin for frenchkids?

Another plays with some kind of abacus. One of the beads is a bus. He makes it have a very dramatic accident. Regarde le bus il s'est écrasé! PSCHHHHHHHUUUUUU

17/04/20

Friday morning

Someone smells so fucking bad.

Is that window broken? I ask no one in particular.

A woman sending a text message in front of me. Désolée que je n'étais pas de bonne humeur la prochaine fois j'irai mieux.

We pull to a stop outside a shiny black marble-faced building. Myself reflected in the wall.

Sorry I was in a bad mood I'll be better next time

17/04/15

Friday afternoon

There is a slightly older woman with dyed black hair and a sour expression and I do not give up my seat for her. I've been teaching all day and after that I had my office hours and I have been talking and explaining and showing and giving and illustrating and trying to make connections and I am pregnant whether you see it or not and now I'm bloody well going to sit in this seat thank you very much

22/04/15

Wednesday morning

83 for once. En route to our first ultrasound, they're doing it early to date it – it's
early but not that early. nearly 7 weeks.
they say they might hear a heartbeat. I
just want to see the little lentil-blueberry
on the screen.

22/04/15

Wednesday afternoon

They can't see anything on the ultrasound not a poppyseed not a lentil certainly not a blueberry and now I have to do a blood-test every 24–48 hours to measure my beta hcg numbers. they have to double every day or so for it to be growing right.

The first thing my sister says when I tell her is stay off the internet. Those are the exceptional cases, she says, those are the outliers. You're going to be fine. Stay off the internet. stay off the internet. don't be scared of the outliers.

I didn't want to say – but I've never been an inlier.

22/04/15

Wednesday evening

4467.

24/04/15

Friday afternoon

4918.

25/04/15

Saturday night

It's in the tube, they found it in the tube.
ectopic it's called. that's greek for out of
place. that's greek for what the fuck.

Methotrexate cancer shot taxi home now
we wait for it to bleed

26/04/15

Sunday night

No bleeding, no pain, no symptoms, they're going to have to operate. Not today please I said, can we do it tomorrow, just give me the night. Medical emergency they said, we need to do it now. No medical emergency I said, no bleeding no pain no symptoms, just give me the night. OK but you have to sign this form that says you're crazy.

Form signed taxi home operation tomorrow.

stupid baby, you'd never survive in the world anyway

27/04/15

Monday morning

Taxi. Boulevard Port-Royal. How many times have I gone down this road on the 91 with no idea that one day I'd be admitted to one of these hospitals, examined, probed, that they'd take my blood, my urine, tell me the baby's in the tube and it can't stay there and we can't go on like this.

Lay me down, put me out, take my tube, send me home.

30/04/15

Thursday morning

It hurts to breathe, laugh, cough, sneeze, feels like I'm tearing my abdominal muscles, like my diaphragm is ragged.

The days have come apart. I don't leave the bed. Don't use my phone except to write this. Check email on my laptop. I can't answer any messages though people send nice ones.

I watch television, I lose myself in other people's plot lines, I watch people who exist pretend to be people who don't exist.

02/05/15

Saturday afternoon

The disorientation of not expecting to be here. you plan your journey, you know the route, but even one stop short of where you were headed and there's just no salvaging the day.

well that bus was uncomfortable and there were too many people on it. still it felt like the only way to get to where I thought I was going.

the part I hate is that I don't even know for sure if I wanted a kid. it all got so medical so quickly. people ask when you're going to have one and you say now soon and they're happy to hear it and you're happy to say it and then it all goes wrong and you're the one lying in bed minus an organ. you can't just do these things to make other people happy.

it's time to stop calculating time.

15/05/15

Friday morning

made it to school to give them their final
exam. haven't seen them in weeks. one
asks where I've been, asks right in front of
everyone. we thought you fell down some
stairs they say. I can't bring myself to tell
them. what do you tell them? we'd all just
feel uncomfortable. I read maggie nelson
while they scribble in their blue books

15/05/15

Friday afternoon

Gave the exam to my other class. On my way home I have to get off the bus and sit on a bench. Feels like parts of me are touching parts they're not supposed to.

15/05/15

Friday night

Meeting M for dinner I venture a metro poem, after Jacques Jouet, though I am no poet. What you do is you think of a line when the train is between stations, and hastily jot it down when the train stops. If you change lines, you make a new stanza.

I'm on the mend and on the tube.
An outlier not an inlier, out of place,
    tubular.
A man with a red leather handbag,
    a tote, beautiful, sharp against his
    white collared shirt, his grey sweater,
    his black slacks, his black hair, white
    repettos.
The bag on the man as out of place as an
    embryo in a tube, who's to say what's
    in place on a man.
Or where an embryo should be for that
    matter.
On the Internet the women claim
    conspiracy, accuse the drug
    companies, they want to sell
    more methotrexate, surely in this day
    and age they could move it into the
    right place.
Distract with thoughts of summertime,

on its way, metro posters, 1 trait d'eau
gazeuse
2 volumes d'aperol 3 volumes de
prosecco and they don't mention the
massive olive or the orange wheel.
Stabbed on a stick and thrust into your
drink, in the summertime.
Imagine amputating the grand canal.
You'd be left with no way to get from one
place to another, a stranded egg; make
your home in some tube.

20/05/15

Wednesday morning

Waiting for the 64, Gambetta to the library. At the bus stop a pregnant woman who must almost be due has to thrust her stomach in my face before I notice her; I am too busy recounting to my pregnant friend J how I've been doing, psychologically, since the surgery, and then that stomach in my face. Oh sorry, I didn't see you, I stand up, resentful, thinking I could be pregnant too for all she knows, and then where would we be? but of course the biggest bump gets the seat. Some consolation in thinking that even if I hadn't lost the baby I'd still be standing. But not much. Fuck thefucking pregnant woman I mutter to my friend who knows not to take it the wrong way. fuck you fuck all pregnant women.

21/05/15

Thursday afternoon

64 back to Gambetta. Across from me, a man plays the bongos on his backpack. He's not bad. Check my email. Your baby is now the size of a grape! I really need to cancel this subscription. But I can't just yet. I'd rather think about my baby growing over the next week to the size of a kumquat. I'd rather think about that.

I'm hungry but embarrassed to eat, this isn't the time or the place, you don't eat on the bus, I'm getting a headache, but if I eat someone will sarcastically say to me bon appétit. I don't care I don't care I don't care stop trying to flatter strangers eat your stupid crunchy sesame bar that you bought three months ago the one you keep in your bag in case you get hungry, well you're hungry now, write what you want, do what you want, cause you're hungry and you've given up caring what anyone thinks and isn't that the best way to write, let alone live? Let alone love.

## Line 11 to line 8

Monday 16/11/15

It's a few months later, and I'm a metro commuter now. Today's a bad day. Total crush. My boobs on some girl's arm, my arm in some guy's groin, an orgy of commuters. A bit of fluff escapes from behind my ear and drifts down in front of my face. It tickles my nose and I try to welcome the sensation instead of fighting it. We travel, groping each other blindly, all of us enduring.

The spring was spotted with deaths and near deaths; the loss of my pregnancy, then the death of my mentor, then almost my dog, and finally a woman I never met but spoke to a lot on Facebook. I went to her funeral in the crematorium at Père Lachaise, and stood and cried with her family and friends, feeling like even though I didn't know any of them, I was in the right place, it was the right place to go that day.

The puffy scars from my surgery stood out against my skin, and slowly flattened, and the year got even worse.

The metro is an exercise in closeness that feels unbearable right now. All of us locked up together in a small space thinking of the same thing. I look over my shoulder and there's a woman in the seat behind me reading about the attacks. Longest night of his life, goes the headline above a picture of François Hollande. Rational friends of mine are avoiding the metro at rush hour. A friend who's late to meet me tells me he got off the metro a few stops too soon because he didn't like the look of a guy. We're all jumpy.

A man goes to the ground with his bag and we all look at him. It's awful that our first thought isn't is he ok, but is he going to try to kill us all? How easy it would be to hide an explosive vest under a puffer jacket, its wire disguised as a white headphone cord, the activation device as an iPhone. These are the things we're thinking about, wondering if headphones are explosive devices. We're all in this together but who can we trust?

I've started having panic attacks on the metro. I have to get off a few stops early and walk home.

But I realized the attacks are coming not in the beginning or the middle of the journey, but just as I'm about to get off. I'm not afraid of the train, I'm afraid of the destination. What are we heading towards, stop by stop? What's just down the track? It's enough to make you want to walk everywhere. Slow it all down.

Even if we're not safe on the streets we can go at our own pace.

I find myself looking at the other people in the city with a new care. They're no longer people in my way. I would feel badly if one of you got hurt. I would hurt if you were hurt. I'm sure some of the people who died took this bus, took this train. Sat where I'm sitting. This strapontin. This one. And that one. I wonder how many times I've been on a bus, or on the metro, with any of them. The chances are good.

Ah Paris I want to make it all better, smooth your rumpled pavement, kiss the hot forehead of Sacré-Coeur.

We're going to have to get used to taking the metro again, though it feels so risky, and brings us into a painful proximity. But it's the closeness that will help us through. We're all repeating to ourselves that the chances of it happening to us are very slim. This is a terrible way to live in a community together – hoping that if the worst strikes, it strikes someone else.

In the city we are forever brushing sleeves with our other possible selves. Underground we go shooting through the tunnels trying to survive and be happy. So many books and films about cities take this as their premise: What if we'd made that train we missed by a second? Are we passing our soul mates on the tracks, in the train going the other way? We're learning this in a new way, after the attacks. If we'd had dinner in one place, instead of another. If we'd gone to see that gig, instead of the other. But what if we could turn this fear into the thing that gets us through this terrible time? We pass people in the street every day and we may not meet them for years, if ever. But we might one day – you just never know. And this must be at least one of the most potent meanings of community: potentiality.

A few days before all this happened, I was once again teaching Georges Perec's strange little book *An Attempt at Exhausting a Place in Paris* (1974) in which he records spending three days sitting in the Place Saint-Sulpice trying to write down everything he sees around him – which buses go by, what kinds of cars, what the people and birds are doing, what the cafes are serving, who's drinking which wine with lunch, what the street signs say, if there are nuns, who's carrying a shopping bag, a plank, a crate, etc. It's a poignant inventory of a Paris of the past (before we all filled up every spare moment gazing into the glowing oracles in our hands), full of 2CV cars and tourists with actual cameras instead of phones on selfie sticks. It's also an exercise in noting what Perec can't see, what's just outside his peripheral vision, threatening to undo the whole; 'even when my only goal is just to observe,' he writes (in Marc Lowenthal's translation); 'I don't see what takes place a few meters from me: I don't notice, for example, that cars are parking.' There is so much we miss; none of us can have a total vision, or total understanding, of even just one place in our cities. This is a powerful and humbling thing to be aware of. As a member of the Oulipo – the Workshop of Potential Literature – Perec valued the potential almost above the actual.

But the reason I keep thinking of Perec is because of another essay he wrote the year before that, called 'Approaches to What?', in which he argues that as a culture, we are preoccupied by the 'big event, the untoward, the extra-ordinary*'; the daily newspapers are full of plane crashes and car crashes and tragedies, and totally ignore the daily – the everyday, what Perec calls the 'infra-ordinary'. The attempt to exhaust a place in Paris is an act of cataloguing that is destined

---

* Perec, Georges. "Approaches to What?" in *Species of Spaces*, ed. and trans. by John Sturrock. London: Penguin Classics, 2008, p. 209

to fail, yet what matters is not the importance of what is observed, but its triviality.
The very futility of asking such questions,
he writes, is 'exactly what makes them
just as essential, if not more so, as all the
other questions by which we've tried in
vain to lay hold on our truth.'

The infra-ordinary. The bus, the metro,
the Velib. Everyday ways of getting here
and there.

I often teach Raymond Queneau's epic
*Exercices de Style* in creative writing work-
shops, this amazing book of 99 different
ways to tell the story of a guy on the bus.
Queneau, Perec, Roubaud – Oulipians are
never so happy as when they're on the bus.
And we read their bus stories because they
teach us how to live together, they teach
us our daily encounters are a hundred
thousand billion different stories told by
Parisians over dinner. And their love of
the daily, the zany, the things you think
of when you're busy doing other things,
that's what gets you through. Queneau
wrote that book just three years after
Paris was liberated from the Nazis. That's
not a very long time.

Since that night, all of us here in Paris,
and many people abroad, have been
asking what feel like futile questions, as
we try to grasp someone else's perverted

idea of truth. Why did they do this, why those places, why those people? Might it all happen again? When? Where? How can we avoid this? How can we be safer in our city? Beyond the air strikes that have already started, beyond the think pieces that encase the events, beyond the catastrophe-comparing and victim-blaming that's already flying fast and loose, the answers are eluding us.

Someone wrote somewhere – maybe it was Virginia Woolf? – that peace is only possible when one man holding a gun can imagine that the other man he's facing down, who is also holding a gun, is a human being like he is, with a family who loves him. (I thought it might be in 'Thoughts on Peace in an Air Raid', which I've just reread, looking for it. It isn't.)

Whoever said that, and someone definitely has, I think what they meant is that peace is only possible when both sides acknowledge the enemy's right to an everyday, to the infra-ordinary. And what happened on Friday night was an amputation of that right.

It's the everydayness of the attacks that gets me, that puts up the block I can't think through, or around. These people, they bought those clothes they were wearing, and paid with their bank cards, and had bankers who will close out their accounts, they had electricity bills, they had shaved that day, or not, and they had pimples, and they were coming down with something, and they'd had a fight, and they were watching their weight, and they'd just got the new album, or they wanted to leave early, or they were watching their weight, and some of them had probably made a note to call the vet on Monday because the dog's vaccinations were up, because some of them had pets, just as they all had parents, siblings, friends, teachers, bakers, people to miss them and mourn them, and also neighbors, like us, who didn't know them, who may not know they're specifically gone, who only know that some group of people we've never met stopped living on Friday the 13th of November 2015, while we're still out here, and all we can do is keep doing every day.

Paris is not a ghost town, in spite of what they're saying on the American news. Since the morning after, people (at least in my neighborhood of Belleville) have been out and about, doing the kinds of things Perec noticed in 1974: buying food, drinking in cafes, carrying shopping bags, even (as we did) carrying a digital piano with its pedals and stand half a mile for a friend. We're defiant, but shaky. We can't get over what we've seen, what we've heard, who we've lost, and we don't really want to. But we'll eventually get used to the fact that it happened. It will become part of our daily lives.

Wherever the infra-ordinary is taken away, wherever civilians are targeted, not only in Paris, Perec's manifesto rings true. 'Question your teaspoons,' he urges us. 'What is there under your wallpaper?' he asks. Perec's parents were killed in the Second World War, his father in the army, his mother in a concentration camp. He had firsthand experience of the eruption of evil into the everyday, so while in some ways *An Attempt at Exhausting a Place in Paris* is a comically Parisian text – oh, the French and their wine at lunch – on some level, it is the diary of an orphaned child who can never accept that the world is the way it is. Why is the world put together this way? This *si parisienne* elevation of the ordinary into something compelling knows that in its peripheral vision lurks the menace of evil, and purposefully, radically chooses to focus, instead, on the fabric of peace.

As I weave and dodge my way through the tunnels at République, changing from the line 11 to the line 8, overtaking the unhurried or inhibited, I notice a man walking in the opposite direction from a ways off, holding his hand up above his head, in the form of a peace sign.

## Epilogue

17/03/21

It's taken me a few years to consider these notes as a book, instead of – I don't know, notes toward an essay, or just some observations on my phone. Something about being yanked out of the public sphere, and resituated, inescapably, in the private sphere, made me want to revisit this text, which is so steeped in the outside world, and to think about whether it might take a more public shape.

Maybe it was the way we all – well, the writers among us anyway – responded by writing up our lockdown diaries, a form that is a close cousin to this bus diary. But mainly I was nostalgic, I think – weren't we, aren't we, all – for public transport in all its fleshy reality, for the days of sharing space and air with strangers. It seems incredible that it was ever what we did; it seems incredible, equally, that it no longer is. How long will it be until we don't have to wear masks? Until we no longer flinch when someone gets a little too close to us?

Current events in France also brought me back to this book. In the fall of 2020, the

Charlie Hebdo trials began in Paris, and with them, the violence returned, extreme barbarism igniting a culture war in which the Republican value of *laïcité* (secularism) clashed with a growing social justice movement. These events, in the middle of a devastating pandemic itself following on from a year of Gilet jaunes protests and massive strikes, have combined to make it a very trying time to live in Paris. And I find myself wondering whether the unity that the Charlie Hebdo demonstrations tapped into is still there.

Despite our political differences, we marched together in January 2015 because it felt healing to be together, in such large numbers, in public. At so many points in our modern history, Parisians have banded together against a perceived common enemy, from the revolutions of the eighteenth and nineteenth centuries, to the Commune, to the Front Populaire, the Liberation, May 1968, and the riots of 1995. I'd like to think that we are bound by this history; that we are included in its collective, no matter where we're from or when we got there. That the moments of history which shatter our everyday are moments to redefine our togetherness.

The rest of the time, we're engrossed in our phones, same as anyone else, anywhere else.

## • Editor's note •

The excerpt from *Ghost Image* by Hervé Guibert is from Robert Bononno's translation, published by University of Chicago Press, 2014


## • Acknowledgments •

Thank you to the following people who helped make this book possible in one way or another, whether they knew it or not:

Amanda Dennis, Hedi El Kholti, Seb Emina, Annie Ernaux, Ben Hackbarth, Heidi Julavits, Chris Kraus, Stephanie La Cava, Deborah Levy, Sarah Manguso, Željka Marosevic, Cécile Menon, Georges Perec, Derek Ryan, Ileene Smith, Joanna Walsh, Alba Ziegler-Bailey, my parents, my sister, and all my anonymous fellow bus-riding Parisians.

Some parts of the final essay were previously published on Literary Hub, so thank you to Jonny Diamond, Michele Filgate for putting me in touch with Jonny, and John Freeman.

• Founded in 2014, **Les Fugitives** is an independent literary press for contemporary fiction and creative non-fiction translated from the French, published for the first time in the UK. **Lauren Elkin** is the first Anglophone author published by Les Fugitives to date. •

Also published by Les Fugitives:

*Eve out of Her Ruins*
*The Living Days*
by **Ananda Devi**
trans. Jeffrey Zuckerman

*This Tilting World*
by **Colette Fellous**
trans. Sophie Lewis
foreword by Michèle Roberts

*Now, Now, Louison*
*Nativity*
by **Jean Frémon**
trans. Cole Swensen

*Translation as Transhumance*
by **Mireille Gansel**
trans. Ros Schwartz
foreword by Lauren Elkin

*A Respectable Occupation*
by **Julia Kerninon**
trans. Ruth Diver
foreword by Lauren Elkin

*Little Dancer Aged Fourteen*
by **Camille Laurens**
trans. Willard Wood

*Blue Self-Portrait*
*Poetics of Work*
by **Noémi Lefebvre**
trans. Sophie Lewis

*Suite for Barbara Loden*
*The White Dress*
by **Nathalie Léger**
trans. Natasha Lehrer

*Exposition*
by **Nathalie Léger**
trans. Amanda DeMarco

*The Governesses*
*The Fool and Other Moral Tales*
by **Anne Serre**
trans. Mark Hutchinson

*Selfies*
by **Sylvie Weil**
trans. Ros Schwartz

• www.lesfugitives.com •

• This first English-language edition published in
the United Kingdom in September 2021 by Les
Fugitives and in United States of America by
Semiotext(e) • Reprinted by Les Fugitives in
November 2021 • Les Fugitives Ltd,
91 Cholmley Gardens, Fortune Green Road,
London NW6 1UN • *www.lesfugitives.com* •
Title page illustration and design by Sarah
Schulte • Text design and typesetting by
MacGuru Ltd • Cover photograph by
Lauren Elkin • Cover design by Brendan Lownds •
All rights reserved • No part of this publication
may be reproduced, stored in a retrieval system or
transmitted in any form or by any means,
electronic, mechanical, photocopying, recording
or otherwise, without prior permission in writing
from Les Fugitives editions • A CIP catalogue
record for this book is available from the British
Library • The right of Lauren Elkin to be identified
as author of this work has been identified in
accordance with Section 77 of the Copyright,
Designs and Patents Act 1988 Printed in England
by TJ Books, Padstow, Cornwall •
ISBN 978-1-8380141-8-6 •